Living Like Je

MW01714081

Challenging the Next Generation to Greater Things in Christ

by

Thomas Ewald, MDiv

Carson-Dellosa Christian Publishing
Greensboro, North Carolina

It is the mission of Carson-Dellosa Christian Publishing to create the highest-quality Scripture-based children's products that teach the Word of God, share His love and goodness, assist in faith development, and glorify His Son, Jesus Christ.

". . . teach me your ways so I may know you. . . ."
Exodus 33:13

Credits

Editor........................... Pamela Holley–Bright
Layout Design............. Mark Conrad
Inside Illustrations...... Julie Anderson
Cover Design............... Peggy Jackson
Cover Illustration......... Russ Flint

ISBN: 978-1-59441-780-1

Table of Contents

Introduction

Living His Way

What does it mean to be a Christian? The name "Christian" gives us an idea, for it means "Christ-like." Instead of guessing what we can do to be a good Christian, we can look to the Person who gave us the example of how a true Christian should act—like Jesus.

Jesus came to save the world from sin and reconcile man with God. He dedicated His life to serving, healing, and teaching others about God's love and faithfulness. We are called to live like Jesus by walking in the way of the Lord. However, living this lifestyle is a challenge.

Each chapter is divided into three sections. The first section defines the attribute of Jesus. It gives the teacher talking points for introducing a characteristic of Jesus to students to help them learn how to be Christlike.

Living the Word

The second section is a dramatization of an event in Jesus's life. It illustrates how He lived the holy life that God calls us to live. While true to the biblical text, it is a dramatization that brings the moment to life in a way that children will be able to grasp—understanding how truly good Jesus is.

Living the Challenge

The third section is a set of challenges. After we have chosen to follow Jesus Christ, we will face many challenges such as temptation and persecution. Jesus was faced with temptation (Luke 4:1–13) and persecution by the very ones who saw Him perform many miracles (Matthew 27:15–26). Jesus fought temptation and persecution not with the swing of a mighty sword, but with the mighty Word of God.

To live like Jesus is to keep the faith in the everyday Christian walk despite the many challenges we will face. With this book, children will learn how to grow strong in Christ. They will also learn how they, too, can challenge themselves to live like Jesus.

Consecrated to God

The word "consecrate" is probably not one that children use in everyday conversations, but it is nevertheless a concept they are familiar with. For example, they know that certain clothes are for school or church only; maybe there are rooms in their homes that are used only when company comes. Perhaps there are certain foods that are served on special occasions.

To consecrate something means to make it special by setting it apart for a certain purpose. In a spiritual sense, that which we set apart becomes holy. We should set ourselves apart and live lives holy unto God just as Jesus did.

Jesus was baptized by John the Baptist to outwardly show that He was setting Himself apart from the world. Your church may practice infant baptism or have a day for dedicating newborns or small children. Both are a way of indicating the desire to be set apart for God.

Maybe your church practices believer's baptism, in which people present themselves to God. Once you have chosen to dedicate your life to the Lord and have chosen to follow His Word, you should show others that you've chosen to walk in the path of righteousness. However, you can also show others you are set apart by how you live—serving God, studying His Word, and sharing God's love with others.

Whether or not children have been baptized as infants, children need to understand that *they* need to make the decision themselves to follow Christ. They should dedicate their lives to Him no matter what others in their families may have done. They need to go to God and say, "This life is yours."

Making the choice to follow God is the ultimate way of recognizing that though we can say, think and do as we wish, we have been created by God and for God's purposes. We are not created to be selfish with our belongings. We are not even created to be selfish with our lives.

Share with children that they are called to do great things, such as healing, teaching, serving, and so much more in the name of the Lord. When they choose to follow His Word and live only for Him, they will be rewarded with eternal life with Him in heaven. But first, they have to make the decision for themselves to choose Him as their Lord and Savior. It is the first step of choosing to live like Jesus!

Dedicated to God

Learn more in: Exodus 13:2, Luke 2:21–40, Matthew 3:1–17, and John 3:16.

Assign readers for the characters listed below.

Narrator

Simeon

Joseph

Mary

John the Baptist

Jesus

Voice from heaven

Narrator: For many years, the people of Israel had waited for the Messiah to arrive. When He finally came, He came in the form of a baby named Jesus.

(Scene One: A great temple in Jerusalem)

Simeon: Oh God, how long must we wait for our Messiah? Your Holy Spirit told me I would not die until I saw Him with my own eyes, but I am getting so old.

Narrator: Just then, Mary and Joseph approached Simeon in the temple with their newborn son.

Joseph: We have come to present our son to God.

Mary: God told Moses that every firstborn male is to be dedicated to Him.

Joseph: And, Jesus is our firstborn.

Mary: So, we bring Him here with our sacrifices—

Joseph: —and our promise that our son will serve God His whole life.

Simeon: He will do so much more than that. I see something special in Him. May I hold Him?

Narrator: Simeon cradled the baby Jesus in his arms and cried out to God.

Simeon: God, Your promise has come true! I now see Your salvation, the Messiah, in this young child.

Joseph: Mary, listen to what he is saying!

Simeon: You marvel at my words, but this child is destined to cause the falling and rising of many in Israel and to be a sign that will be spoken against.

Narrator: Joseph and Mary left the temple and took Jesus home to Nazareth. There, Jesus grew and was filled with wisdom and the grace of God was upon Him.

(Scene Two: The Jordan River)

Narrator: Thirty years later, a man preached in the desert of Judea. He wore clothing made of camel's hair with a leather belt tied around his waist. He urged everyone to repent of their sins and to be baptized. His name was John the Baptist. He was the one who prepared the way for Jesus Christ.

John the Baptist: Repent, for the kingdom of heaven is near! I baptize with water, but One is coming who is much greater than I. He will baptize with the Holy Spirit!

Narrator: Jesus approached John to be baptized.

John the Baptist: It's You! Why do You come to me, when it is I who needs to be baptized by You?

Jesus: I must be baptized in order to fulfill all righteousness. I am obedient to God and will always do His will.

Narrator: So, John baptized Jesus. Jesus dedicated Himself to God in the waters of the Jordan River. Suddenly, the sky opened and the Spirit of God descended on Jesus. Then, there was a voice from heaven.

Voice from heaven: This is my Son, whom I love and with whom I am well pleased!

Narrator: Jesus lived His life in obedience to God's will—just as you and I can do.

Challenges

Prayer Mobile

Just as baptism is a way to dedicate ourselves to God, we can also dedicate our days to Him. This activity will help children remember to dedicate their days to the Lord.

Morning Dedication Prayer

Each day, we can make the decision to follow God, ignore Him, or turn down another path. Help children create a morning reminder to follow God. Use the sun and cloud patterns (page 9) to create a Prayer Mobile. Children may use the morning prayer below or make up one of their own.

Lord God, I dedicate my life to you this morning.
May all I say and do be for Your glory.

Through my words and actions,
Lord, let me be Your servant today.
Guide me to places and people
Who need to know more about You.

God, take now the life I give to You
And use it this day as you wish. Amen.

Night Dedication Prayer

We are blessed that God watches over us even as we sleep. Sleep is the gift He has given us to strengthen us for the challenges of each new day. Alternatively, children may use the night prayer below with the moon and star patterns (page 9) to create a nighttime Prayer Mobile.

Lord, today I have tried to live completely for You.
There have been times when I did well.
Forgive me for the times I fell short.

Watch over me as I sleep tonight and give me rest.
Strengthen me so that tomorrow I may
Walk in Your way and do Your will. Amen.

Materials Needed:

- Heavy, white 11" x 17" (30 cm x 43 cm) paper
- Crayon, markers, glitter
- Single-hole punch
- Glue/clear tape
- Patterns (page 9)
- Scissors
- Fishing line/string

Directions for both dedication prayer mobiles:

1. Enlarge the Prayer Mobile patterns (page 9) by 154% and copy onto heavy, white 11" x 17" (30 cm x 43 cm) paper. *Note: You will only need one copy of the sun and moon patterns, but make three to five copies of the cloud and star patterns. Children will write the prayers inside them.*
2. Have children write out their prayers. Use crayons, markers, or glitter to decorate the patterns. Then, cut out the patterns.
3. Punch out the black spots on the patterns.
4. Attach the cloud patterns to the sun pattern and the star patterns to the moon pattern by threading fishing line or string through the holes at the top of each pattern.
5. Pull the fishing line taut. On the backside of the pattern, glue or place clear tape over the fishing line to hold it in place.
6. Make a loop in the fishing line at the top of both the sun and moon patterns. These loops will be used to hang the mobiles.

Prayer Mobile Patterns

A Student of Scripture

"In the beginning was the Word, and the Word was with God, and the Word was God." John 1:1

Jesus was a student of Scripture. It is easy to forget since it is His birth, life, death, and resurrection that the Old Testament prophets wrote about. Yet, Jesus studied Scripture as He grew up.

In Luke 2:46, Joseph and Mary find Jesus in the temple "sitting among the teachers, listening to them and asking them questions." Jesus was filled with wisdom, even as a young child (Luke 2:40). As He was asking questions and listening to the teachers, the Bible says all were amazed at His understanding (Luke 2:47). As an adult, Jesus is seen again in the synagogue (Luke 4:14–20). The difference is that Jesus, who grew up learning the Scriptures, is now a teacher and able to show how He is the fulfillment of the Scriptures (Luke 4:21).

To be like Jesus also means to honor the truth of God's Word. We learn the Word by reading it, studying it, and knowing how Jesus embodied the promises God made. Teach children that they can grow in understanding by reading the Word, asking questions, and living by God's promises.

Jesus Himself asked questions. It is important to study God's Holy Word so that we can more fully understand it. When we study the Word, we can also teach and lead others to Christ.

Just as Jesus studied, questioned, and taught others the truth of the Scriptures, children can grow in their wisdom of God's Word by being like Jesus—a student of Scripture.

Jesus in the Temple

Learn more in Luke 2:41–51.

Assign readers for the characters listed below.

Narrator

Mary

Joseph

Jesus

Narrator: Passover has ended and many people who traveled to Jerusalem for the festival are leaving for their homes. For some, it is a journey of many days. Among the travelers are Mary and Joseph, the parents of a 12-year-old boy named—

Mary: Jesus! Joseph, do you know where Jesus is?

Joseph: I don't know. I figured you did.

Mary: Perhaps He is with some of our relatives.

Joseph: Or with some of His friends.

Mary: Joseph, I'm worried. Let's find Him before we go any further.

Narrator: Mary and Joseph looked for Jesus but did not find Him with their relatives, His friends or with anyone in the crowds of travelers.

Mary: We must return to Jerusalem; He is probably still there!

Narrator: So, Mary and Joseph returned to Jerusalem and looked all over for Jesus.

Joseph: Mary, it's been three days! We've looked everywhere. Where has that boy gone to?

Mary: I don't know, but we must keep looking.

Joseph: Look over there, Mary, in the temple. Isn't that Him?

Mary: No, that must be one of the students talking to His teachers. Probably a smart little boy. Wait! That's no student, that's my son!

Joseph: Like I said.

Mary: Jesus! Jesus!

Jesus: Mother!

Mary: We have been looking everywhere for you!

Joseph: How could you just go off without asking?

Jesus: But, why did you search so hard? Didn't you realize I would be in my Father's house?

Narrator: Though they were relieved to find Him, Joseph and Mary did not understand what Jesus meant by "my Father's house." But, Jesus was telling them that He wanted to learn more about His relationship with His Heavenly Father, God.

Mary: Come with us now, Jesus. It is time to go home.

Narrator: As they resumed their journey out of Jerusalem, Mary treasured all that had happened in her heart.

Challenges

Scripture Journal

Have children keep Scripture Journals. These books will be in addition to any other materials they use for learning in the classroom. Journals can be spiral notebooks or something assembled in class.

During each class time, focus on two Scriptures used in the lesson. Have children write the line(s) of Scripture in their journals, including the book of the Bible, chapter, and verse where each can be found. Then, have them record what a particular verse means to them. Finally, guide children in their discussion of the verses, referring to Bible commentaries, study Bibles, or other people in your congregation for help with explanations as needed.

When they are studying the Bible at home, have children take notes in their journals on what they read. Encourage them to write about ways they could share this Scripture with others or to make a prayer list of the people God brings to their minds when they are reading the Scripture. Of course, these are only a couple of suggestions. Explain to children that their journals are for their own personal reflections, prayers, responses, and learning of God's Word. By the end of the school year, their Scripture Journals will almost be filled. Tell students how important it is not only to read the Word, but to always reflect on it and apply it to their lives. Encourage them to keep up the habit of writing in their journals even after you've reached the end of the school year.

Students in the Temple

Suggest that children take their Scripture Journals with them to worship. Have them to take notes and write down any questions they may have on the sermon. As a class, discuss the following questions: What did they learn from the sermon? What questions did they have? How will they live out what they've learned?

One student could act as the teacher and share the sermon with the entire class. Students could bring in visuals such as pictures or clippings from magazines and newspapers to discuss how to apply the sermon to their everyday lives.

Then, divide the class into groups or pairs. Encourage students to share their views, questions, and thoughts on what they've learned in recent sermons. Let students try to answer each other's questions. If they still have unanswered questions, tell them to pray and ask God for the answers *For the LORD gives wisdom, and from his mouth come knowledge and understanding.* Proverbs 2:6

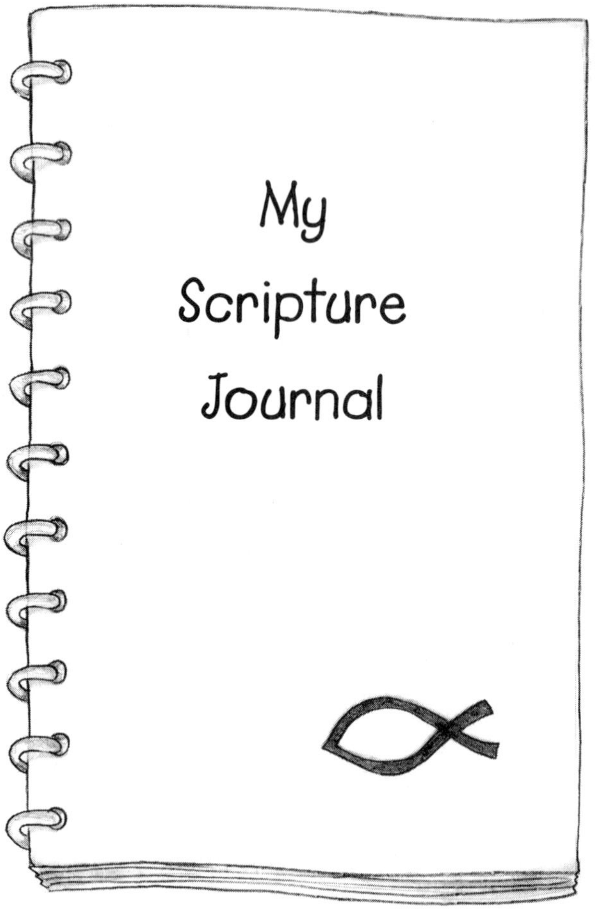

Trusting in God

What does it mean to trust God? The Bible is filled with promises of hope, forgiveness, comfort, guidance, provisions, and love. Yet, trusting does not come easily. How do we know that God will take care of us?

In His preaching, Jesus gives us an illustration of why we can trust God for care: . . . *do not worry about your life, what you will eat or drink, or about your body, what you will wear. Is not life more important than food, and the body more important than clothes? Look at the birds of the air; they do not sow or reap or store away in barns, and yet your heavenly Father feeds them. Are you not much more valuable than they?* (Matthew 6:25–26) If God takes care of the birds, He will surely take care of us. However, we must place our trust—our firm belief—in His Word and promise to take care of us.

To trust God means to have faith in Him. *Now faith is being sure of what we hope for and certain of what we do not see.* (Hebrews 11:1) In other words, even though we can't physically see God, we know He's there and we can be assured of His love for us, His presence in our lives through His Word, and His promise that He will take care of all of our needs.

The Bible provides a powerful example of Jesus's faith in God: He trusted that God would take care of Him when He fasted in the desert. After Jesus fasted for 40 days and 40 nights, Satan went to the desert to tempt Him. Satan even tried to get Jesus to turn away from God so that Jesus would worship him (Matthew 4:9). After Satan left Jesus, God sent His angels to attend to Him (Matthew 4:11).

Jesus trusted in the power of the Word and trusted that His father would care for Him. Trusting God is a great way to demonstrate faith in Him. Share with children the importance of trusting in God just as Jesus did.

Jesus in the Desert

Learn more in Matthew 4:1–11, Mark 1:12–13, and Luke 4:1–13.

Assign readers for the characters listed below.

Narrator

John's Follower 1

John's Follower 2

John's Follower 3

Satan

Jesus

Narrator: After He was baptized by John the Baptist, Jesus was led by the Holy Spirit into the desert.

John's Follower 1: Hey, where did Jesus go?

John's Follower 2: He went into the desert.

John's Follower 3: But He took nothing with Him but the clothes on His back. He took no food or water or anything else for that matter that a person would take on a trip into such a dangerous place.

John's Follower 1: He will never survive the night. Is He crazy?

John's Follower 2: No, He knows that God will take care of him.

John's Follower 3: That takes guts.

John's Follower 2: No, it takes faith.

Narrator: Jesus did more than survive the night. He survived 40 days and 40 nights of fasting.

Jesus: I have been here for a long time. I'm hungry and I'm thirsty.

Narrator: Not only that, but the desert was filled with wild beasts. Suddenly, a voice spoke to Jesus.

Satan: Oh, Je—sus.

Jesus: Who is it?

Satan: Jesus, is this what God wants for you—that you should starve in the desert? If you are the Son of God, just tell these stones to turn to bread.

Jesus: It is written, "One does not live by bread alone but by every word that comes from the mouth of God."

Satan: Come with me Jesus, there is something I want to show you.

Narrator: Just then, Jesus and Satan were standing at the top of the Temple in the holy city.

Satan: If you are the Son of God, throw yourself off this Temple. Doesn't God promise in the Scriptures that He will command His angels to protect you?

Jesus: Don't you know that it is written, "Do not put the Lord Your God to the test?"

Narrator: Suddenly, the Temple was gone, and Satan stood with Jesus on top of a mountain.

Satan: Look, Jesus. See all of the kingdoms of the world below you. Look at how beautiful they are.

Narrator: Indeed, the view was beautiful, and what power the ruler of all of these kingdoms would have! Satan made an offer.

Satan: Jesus, all I ask is that you fall down and worship me. In return, I will give you everything you can see— all of the kingdoms, all of the splendor.

Jesus: It is written, "Worship the Lord your God and serve Him only." I refuse to worship you, Satan. Now, go away!

Narrator: Satan then left Him. Jesus trusted that God would take care of Him while He fasted. When Satan came to tempt Him away from fasting, Jesus trusted in God's Word to guard Him from His enemy. God even sent His angels to comfort Jesus after He finished His fast.

Challenges

Power Scripture

Jesus knew what He was doing in the desert. Instead of trying to argue with Satan, He quoted Scripture, and Satan was defeated. What a wonderful concept to explain to children! Like Jesus, they can also trust the truth and strength in God's Word and use it not just in times of temptation, but anytime they are feeling fear, anger, hurt, and loneliness.

Help children to create a collection of Power Scriptures that they can turn to in times of need. Use a concordance or a topical Bible to look up verses for these and other subjects: loneliness, anger, sadness, fear, etc. Then, help children write the subject and verse on note cards like this:

When I Am Scared
Even though I walk through the valley of the shadow of death, I will fear no evil, for you are with me; your rod and your staff, they comfort me. Psalm 23:4

Have them keep these cards together in a box or in an envelope. Children can also write their Power Scriptures in their Scripture Journals (page 12). Now, they will have reminders that they can use the power of God's Word and put their trust in Him in *any* situation!

Care Offering

Do this quick activity on a regular basis. Ask children to write something they are concerned about on a piece of paper. It could be a family issue, a friendship problem, or a community or world concern. Then, ask children to fold their papers in half, place their concerns in a basket that you pass through the class.

Tell children that just as we give our tithes and offerings to God, we also give Him our cares, trusting that He will provide for us in our time of need. Ask them to picture their particular concerns in God's hands now. As a class, pray over the basket.

The care offering can also be done at home. Encourage children to do this activity with their families.

Give Up What?!

No doubt, some of the children will be amazed that Jesus went 40 days and 40 nights without food or water. They will be amazed, not because Jesus could do amazing things, but because many of them couldn't imagine a day going by without a favorite snack or activity.

Explain to the class that Jesus demonstrated faith in God's provision in the desert. God did provide strength, comfort, and power to defeat Satan. In the same way, we can trust God to provide for needs in our lives.

Challenge children to trust that God will meet their needs this week. Have them name a snack or activity that they will go without until you get together again. Reassure them that they don't need to rely on these things to provide a life that is filled with joy.

The next time you get together, ask children how many followed through on the challenge and what they gave up. Encourage them to share with the class what it felt like to go without their favorite food or activity. How did they see God providing happiness for them in other ways?

A Disciple Maker

Jesus called an initial group of followers whom He would teach, and they became His disciples. Disciples are followers of Christ, those who are committed to His ways and to preaching the good news of salvation. Jesus taught the first disciples about the Kingdom of God, but He also showed them miraculous things. The more they lived around Jesus, the more they grew in their faith in Him. Each of us, too, can teach people about the Kingdom of God, show them a Christlike life, and spread God's Word.

No one is under qualified. Jesus called laborers and outcasts, not religious big shots or political powerhouses. Though, if he did, they probably would have been good disciples as well. In fact, the Bible tells us that the religious leader Nicodemus became a follower of Jesus after meeting Him one night and asking Him, "But, how can one be born a second time?" (John 3:1–20)

The stories of the disciples throughout the entire New Testament should remind us of two things—first, that God calls all of us to follow Him. There is no one to whom this call does not extend. Even Saul of Tarsus, a persecutor of Christians, was called. He became Paul, one of the greatest disciples, after he opened his heart to the Lord.

Second, the stories should remind us that we are also called to go out into the world and make disciples (Matthew 28:19–20). In this way, knowledge of God's love spreads all around the world, from generation to generation, and we get to be a part of God's plan! Jesus was devoted to seeing God's love reach all people. We, too, are called to spread God's love and the news of salvation to others.

Jesus Calls the Disciples

Learn more in Matthew 4:18–22, Mark 1:16–20, Luke 5:2–11, and John 1:35–50

Assign readers for the characters listed below.

Narrator

Peter

Andrew

Jesus

Philip

Nathanael

Narrator: Jesus came to save the world from its sins and to tell people that God loved them very much. But, He knew His work could also be done by teaching others to follow in His footsteps. That way His work would continue even after He returned to heaven. He began His search not in the Temple or synagogues but among regular people who lived along the Sea of Galilee.

Peter: Hey, Andrew, pay attention and help me cast this net into the water. We earn our pay by catching fish, not by standing in boats and doing nothing.

Andrew: I hear you; it's just that I think that man over there is calling to us. Listen.

Jesus: Allow me to come into your boat so that I may teach this crowd about the Kingdom of God!

Narrator: Peter and Andrew did as Jesus said and took the boat farther into the water so that everyone on shore could see and hear Jesus. When He was done teaching, Jesus turned His attention to Peter and Andrew.

Jesus: Put the boat into deeper water and cast your nets, and you will catch fish.

Peter: Impossible. We have been fishing all night and have caught nothing. But, if you say so, I will do it.

Andrew: Hold on, Peter! I'm already feeling like we've got some!

Peter: Pull the net up, brother.

Andrew: I am, but, it's so full, I'm afraid the net will break!

Peter: We need some help with this catch, or our boat will sink. Call the others.

Andrew: James, John, bring your boat over here! We've got more fish than we can handle!

Peter: Jesus, you must go away from me for I am a sinful man.

Jesus: Don't be afraid, Peter. From now on, you and your brother will follow me, and you will catch people instead of fish.

Narrator: The fishermen pulled ashore and Peter and Andrew followed Jesus. Even James and John left their father to follow him. As they continued on their journey, Jesus called more followers.

Jesus: Philip, follow me!

Philip: I will follow you, Jesus, and I know someone else who will, too. Nathanael!

Nathanael: What is it, Philip?

Philip: It's Him—the One we have heard about from Moses and from the prophets! His name is Jesus, and He is from Nazareth. Come, see!

Nathanael: Nazareth? Can anything good come from there?

Jesus: I see an honest man before me.

Nathanael: How could you possibly know me?

Jesus: I saw you sitting under the fig tree before Philip even called to you.

Nathanael: You are the Son of God!

Jesus: Nathanael, you call me that just because I saw you sitting under a fig tree? Follow me; I will show you greater things than that.

Narrator: And, Jesus did show them and the other disciples that joined them greater things. He showed them that God so loved the world that He sent His Son to us—Jesus of Nazareth.

Challenges

Little Disciples

God gave us some powerful instructions. It is our duty as disciples to witness to people about our Lord and Savior, Jesus Christ. Explain to children that people will have questions about living for God. Below are a few examples. Following are verses children can use to respond to the questions.

- "Does Jesus really love me?" *This is how we know what love is: Jesus Christ laid down his life for us.* (1 John 3:16) What amazing love Jesus has for us! Jesus gave His life so that we may have eternal life with Him in heaven. There is no greater love.
- "Will I be able to do the things I do now?" *No one can serve two masters. Either he will hate the one and love the other, or he will be devoted to the one and despise the other."* (Matthew 6:24) Giving your life to the Lord does mean giving up your old ways. But, once you choose salvation, you will be filled with the new joy that comes from His Word and from His love, faithfulness, and goodness to us.
- "I've made wrong choices. Will God want anything to do with me?" *Therefore, if anyone is in Christ, he is a new creation; the old has gone, the new has come!* (2 Corinthians 5:17) God is always willing to forgive you. Once you give your life over to Him, everything you did before is put in the past, and you can start a new life.

We have to be able to answer the questions people have about living like Jesus. Encourage children to use God's Word to respond to questions when witnessing to others—just like Jesus did.

Share Your Testimony

When did children repent of their sins and choose to live new lives in Christ? Ask them to share their testimonies by making scrapbook pages. They should use anything that reflects who they were before they became followers of Christ. They should also have items that represent their lives as followers of Christ. Children can bring in pictures (or they may choose to draw and decorate their own pictures), small items that can easily be attached to the page (for example, stickers, buttons, bracelets, pins, etc.) Next, have them write their stories and share verses that reflect their experience. Encourage the children to use their own testimonies when witnessing to others.

Make Disciples—Just Two

"Therefore go and make disciples of all nations, baptizing them in the name of the Father and of the Son and of the Holy Spirit, and teaching them to obey everything I have commanded you." Matthew 28:19–20

Using their testimony pages and the verses they've learned from the Little Disciples activity, challenge children to witness to two people in class about Jesus dying for our sins, so that we might have everlasting life with Him in Paradise. To help them when they're witnessing, children can create Salvation Booklets.

Like the Scripture Journals (page 12), Salvation Booklets can also be created by using spiral notebooks or assembled using other materials. Tell children to place their testimony pages and the verses from the Little Disciples activity in their Salvation Booklets. They should then share their Salvation Booklets when they are witnessing to two of their classmates.

The next time you meet as a class, have children share their experience with the rest of the class. After everyone has shared his experience, pray together that God will provide opportunities for witnessing.

In Conversation with God

God created us, giving us the very breath that fills our lungs and fuels our speech. He gave us hearts that feel and minds that think great thoughts. How fitting then that we should use these gifts to communicate with the Creator Who gave these things to us.

Jesus worshiped at the synagogue and grew up with prayer in His life. Even though He was God's Son, He used prayer and worship to communicate with His Father in Heaven. Jesus showed us what it means to live a life in conversation with God. Throughout His ministry, as recorded in the Gospels, Jesus is frequently seen praying alone. In Mark 6:45–47, Jesus goes to a mountainside to pray by himself. He is also praying alone before His arrest in the Garden of Gethsemane (Matthew 26:36–39). God also listens to our prayers, which means He is in conversation with us. What remarkable access we have to our Creator!

While teaching children the importance of prayer, also teach the importance of refraining from "showboat prayer." Jesus says, *"when you pray, do not be like the hypocrites, for they love to pray standing in the synagogues and on the street corners to be seen by men. . . . But when you pray, go into your room, close the door and pray to your Father, who is unseen. Then your Father, who sees what is done in secret, will reward you."* Matthew 6:5–6

We don't need to prove to others that we pray. What is important is that God knows our prayers. He is with us when we pray, listening to everything we say and is ready to take care of anything that we ask for, as long as what we ask for is in His perfect will. Jesus said that "If you believe, you will receive whatever you ask for in prayer." Matthew 21:22

Though Jesus spoke against being a show-off in any of our spiritual practices (Matthew 6:5–10), His personal prayer life naturally caught the attention of the disciples. They wanted to know how they, like Jesus, could enter into conversation with God. The prayer He taught them is still used today all over the world when people pray: "Our Father, Who art in Heaven. . ."

Jesus prayed to show His obedience to and relationship with God. We should all have conversations with God. When we awaken in the morning and go to bed at night, we should acknowledge His presence and pray that His will be done. Children are already like Jesus in this respect—they have a Father in Heaven who is ready and willing to speak with them at anytime.

Jesus in Prayer

Learn more in Matthew 6:1–15 and Luke 11:1–13.

Assign readers for the characters listed below.

Narrator

Disciple 1

Disciple 2

Disciple 3

Jesus

Narrator: Everywhere Jesus went, the disciples followed. They traveled together, they ate together, and they slept in the same place. But, there were times when Jesus would go off by Himself. These were times when He needed to be alone in the presence of His Father, God.

Disciple 1: Look at Jesus. Everyday, He goes off by Himself. What does He do?

Disciple 2: I know what He does. He goes to pray to God.

Disciple 3: But, it is more like He is having a conversation with God.

Disciple 2: I wonder what He is saying to God.

Disciple 1: Perhaps there is something to praying. I bet we could talk to God like Jesus does.

Disciple 3: Maybe we should ask Him.

Disciple 2: John taught his followers how to pray.

Disciple 3: I'm sure Jesus would teach us.

Disciple 1: Here He comes, let's ask Him.

Disciple 2: Jesus, Teacher, would you teach us how to pray?

Jesus: Of course. Remember this, praying is like giving to the needy or fasting; these are things to be done for God, not so that people will see you and think "Oh, look, what a holy person." When you pray, you are praying to talk to God, not to show people how holy you are.

Disciple 3: I don't understand.

Jesus: Some people love to pray standing where they are sure to be seen by others. That is what they want. So, when they receive their attention, they are receiving their reward, as well.

Disciple 1: But, they are so holy.

Disciple 2: You mean they *look* so holy.

Disciple 3: Yeah, who knows how holy they actually are?

Jesus: So, whenever you pray, go away to your room and pray to God. Do not show off when you do it.

Disciple 1: But, some of them pray and pray and pray; they sound so holy.

Disciple 2: Exactly, they *sound* so holy.

Disciple 3: Who knows how holy they actually are?

Jesus: So when you pray, do not keep babbling, hoping that everyone will hear you.

Disciple 2: Then, what should we say?

Jesus: This is how you should pray. Our Father in Heaven, may your name be honored. May your Kingdom come. May what you want to happen be done on Earth as it is done in Heaven. Give us today our daily bread. Forgive us our sins, just as we also have forgiven those who sin against us. Keep us from falling into sin when we are tempted. Save us from the evil one.

Narrator: Then, Jesus went on to tell them more about prayer. Most importantly, He continued to teach them by His example what it was like to be a person who spoke continuously with God in all circumstances.

Challenges

Off on Your Own

Allow the children to exercise the type of personal prayer that Jesus encouraged. Give them each a copy of the Lord's Prayer and have them find quiet places in the classroom to pray it.

When you have called children back together, ask them how they think this prayer—

- helps us. ("May what you want to happen be done on Earth as it is done in Heaven.")
- helps us be better people. ("Forgive us our sins, just as we also have forgiven those who sin against us.")
- helps us get through difficult times. ("Keep us from falling into sin when we are tempted. Save us from the evil one.")

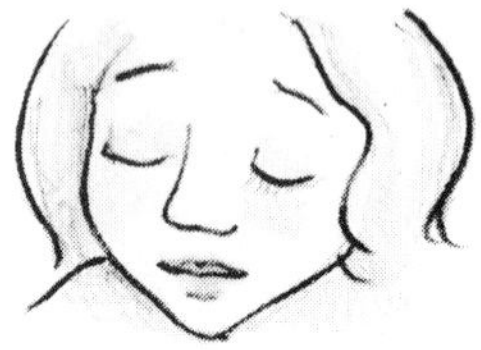

Prayers from the Bible

The Lord's Prayer is not the only model for prayer that the Bible holds for us. The Psalms of David are also prayers that we can apply to our prayer lives as well.

In particular, Psalm 18 is a model of a prayer of faith. Psalm 22 is a model of prayer in times of sorrow, Psalm 102 is a prayer for help, and Psalm 111 is a prayer of thanksgiving.

Group Prayer

Jesus told the disciples to go off on their own and pray. Yet, elsewhere in the Bible, Jesus says, *"Again, I tell you that if two of you on earth agree about anything you ask for, it will be done for you by my Father in heaven. For where two or three come together in my name, there am I with them."* (Matthew 18:19–20)

Jesus said when two or three come together in His name, He's there with them. Put aside time to have a group prayer where children are encouraged to come up with intercessory prayer requests for the needs of others. Make a list of the intercessory prayer requests. Then, give each child a slip of paper with a particular prayer request on it.

Open with something simple, such as "God, we gather together in Jesus's name and ask You to hear the prayers of this class." Form a circle and have each child say the request written on her paper. Close by saying ". . . All of these things we ask of You as we pray the prayer Jesus taught us to pray:

Our Father in heaven, may your name be honored. May your kingdom come. May what you want to happen be done on earth as it is done in heaven. Give us today our daily bread. Forgive us our sins, just as we also have forgiven those who sin against us. Keep us from falling into sin when we are tempted. Save us from the evil one. Matthew 6:9–13 NIrV

This illustrates how individual prayers can come together to form the type of corporate prayer that Jesus encouraged.

A Friend to All People

In a perfect world, it would be easy for everyone to live together in love. After all, we share the same Creator. But, we live in societies that have always been divided by regional, racial, and religious differences. Jesus lived a life that demonstrated that these lines must be crossed if we are going to live lives characterized by the love God tells us to have for one another (John 13:34).

Just like today, the world in Jesus's time was divided by regional, racial, and religious differences. Prejudice existed then as surely as it does now. But, Jesus did not turn a blind eye to it. Instead, He showed love that knew no boundaries. In the story of the Samaritan woman at the well (John 4:5–42), Jesus crosses a social barrier that was a radical move during His time (John 4:9).

What lesson, especially for children, is there in the story of the woman at the well? Love—love freely. Children will experience new social situations as they encounter new grade levels, new schools, and new classmates, to name just a few. In all of these situations, they may experience similar social barriers.

God loves everyone. Jesus talked one-on-one to people to let them know that God loves them. Living like Jesus means loving all people—without barriers—no matter what social differences exist.

The Woman at the Well

Learn more in John 4:5–42

Assign readers for the characters listed below.

Narrator

Jesus

Woman

Narrator: While the disciples went to buy food in the city, Jesus walked along to a town in Samaria where there was a well.

Jesus: It is a hot day, and I am tired from traveling. I think I will rest by this well for a little bit.

Woman: What a hot time of day it is to be dragging water from the well back to my house!

Jesus: Excuse me, I was wondering if, while you are getting water from the well, you would also get me some to drink.

Woman: Sir, you don't want to talk to me, believe me.

Jesus: Why is that?

Woman: Because You are a Jew and I am a Samaritan. Jews do not talk to my people. I just came to get my bucket of water, and I will leave.

Jesus: But, if you knew who I was and the gift from God that I know about, you would not only want me to talk with you. You'd ask me for a drink of water— a drink of living water.

Woman: What? But, You don't have anything to use to get water from the well, and it is a deep well. Tell me, where would You get this living water?

Jesus: Let me tell you more. The people who drink the water that comes from this well will feel good, but, after awhile, they will be thirsty again.

Woman: Of course.

Jesus: But, those who drink the living water that I give them are like people who take a drink of water and never get thirsty again.

Woman: Then, please give me a drink of this water so that I can stop coming to this well every day.

Jesus: I bring a different kind of water than that. It creates something in you that leads to eternal life.

Narrator: The woman did not seem to understand Jesus, so He explained it another way.

Jesus: Do this for me; go get your husband.

Woman: Oh, I don't have a husband.

Jesus: Correct. In fact, even though you have had five husbands, the man you are with now is not your husband.

Woman: You know all about my life! You are surely a prophet. But, again I wonder why do You talk to me? We worship on this mountain, and Jews worship in Jerusalem. Our people do not worship together.

Jesus: There will come a time when what you are called will not matter and where you go to worship will not matter.

Woman: But, how will I worship?

Jesus: God wants you to be a true worshiper. You must present yourself honestly before Him in worship.

Woman: Well, I know a little bit about what you are saying, but the Messiah is coming someday, and He will explain everything to me.

Jesus: I am the Messiah.

Woman: I am glad that You did talk to me! Please, wait here while I tell my people that the Messiah is here!

Narrator: The woman told her people about the man who talked to her even though she was a Samaritan woman.

Woman: Could this really be Him? He knew all about me, and we'd never even met!

Narrator: And, the people of the town came to see the man willing to offer them not just a drink of water, but eternal life!

Challenges

Share: When Did You Feel Left Out?

Everybody can relate to a time when they felt left out. It feels bad when friends play together without you, older siblings close their bedroom doors on you, or parents go to "grown-up" events. It is even worse if there are bad feelings behind these actions.

Encourage children to share times when they felt left out. How did they feel when this happened? How did they overcome these feelings?

Reaching Out

Now, tell children to think of someone they know who has been left out or made to feel like he was not part of a group. Help them think of specific things they can do to reach out to him. Some activities they may want to consider are: inviting him to come over for snacks, planning a sleep over and inviting other friends to introduce them to the new friend, or including him when playing sports or other games.

Maybe there is a new child in your group who feels left out because she has to get used to new people and a new classroom environment. If this is the case, encourage children to welcome her by making a card telling her how glad they are to have her as a classmate. Also, suggest that children take turns inviting her to sit with them during lunch or snack time.

There are many great opportunities for children to reach out to someone and make a new friend. Be sure to follow-up on this activity. See what good stories come from children reaching out to others like Jesus did.

A Teacher

In an earlier lesson, we learned that Jesus, as a young boy, was a student of Scripture. Jesus lived in obedience to God's Word and used the Scriptures in all circumstances.

Luke concludes this account of Jesus's childhood by writing, *And Jesus grew in wisdom and stature, and in favor with God and men.* (Luke 2:52) Jesus didn't take what He learned in the temple and keep it to Himself. Instead, filled with wisdom and the grace of God, He began His ministry to teach others about God's love.

Jesus was a masterful teacher. He taught about the Kingdom of God using stories with imagery that the people could understand. He taught people how to live for God and to love, just as God had first loved them. Today, Jesus's teachings speak to audiences of all ages and circumstances.

To be like Jesus the teacher, we don't have to have a classroom; even one friend will do. We only need to help others learn about Jesus.

Jesus said that "the harvest is ready but the workers are few" (Luke 10:2). We are the workers. There is much to learn about the history of God's relationship with His people. Share with children that we are called to be teachers. In an earlier lesson, they learned how to be disciple makers. Now, children can become teachers, sharing with others what they know about Jesus.

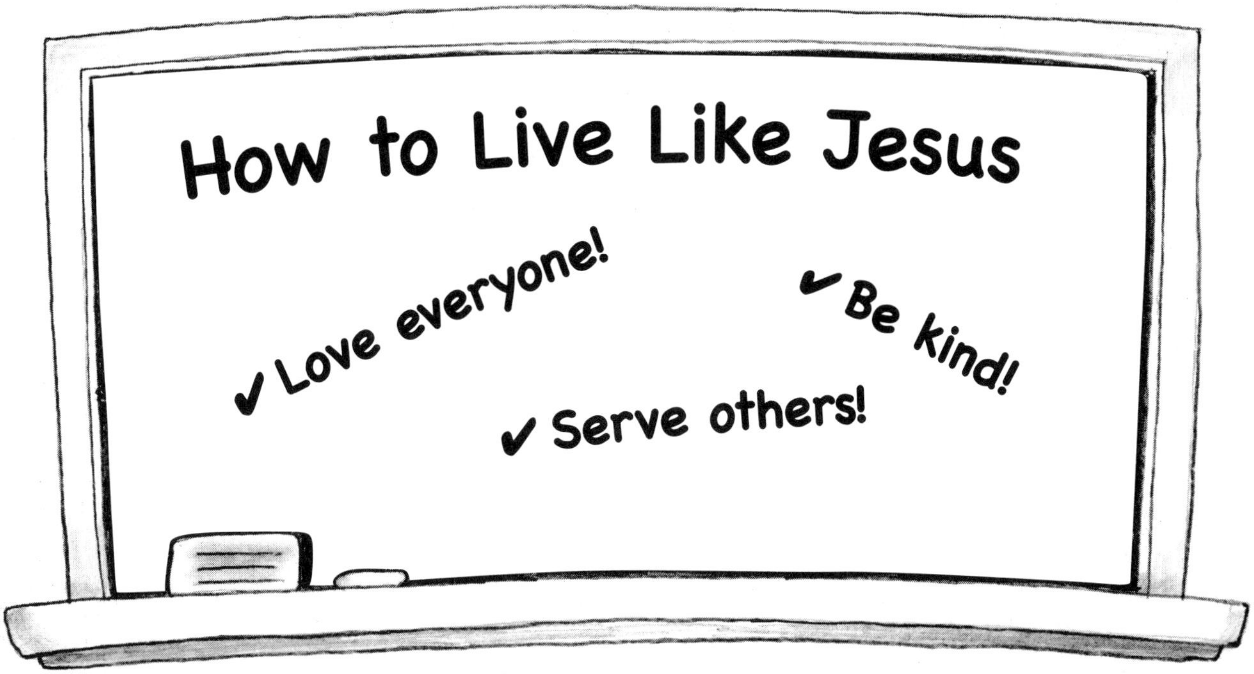

The Sermon on the Mount

Learn more in Matthew 5:1–48 and Luke 6:20–49

Assign readers for the characters listed below.

Narrator

Father

Daughter

Mother

Jesus

Son

Narrator: After being baptized by John the Baptist and spending 40 days in the desert, Jesus immediately began to teach the people about the Kingdom of Heaven.

Father: What did He say? "Blessed are the poor in spirit, for theirs is the Kingdom of Heaven? Blessed are those who mourn for they will be comforted?"

Daughter: Yeah, listen. He's saying, "Blessed are the meek, for they shall inherit the earth, and blessed are those who hunger and thirst for righteousness for they will be filled."

Mother: And, "the merciful will be shown mercy, the pure in heart will see God, and the peacemakers will be called sons of God."

Jesus: Blessed are you when people insult you, persecute you and falsely say all kinds of evil against you because of Me. Rejoice and be glad because great is your reward in Heaven.

Father: He is saying that people like us can be a part of the Kingdom of Heaven. In fact, He is saying it is a kingdom for the poor, the meek, the hungry and thirsty, and the persecuted.

Son: But, what are we supposed to do when the people do all of those bad things and hurt us?

Jesus: Love your enemies, do good to those who hate you, bless those who curse you, pray for those who mistreat you.

Son: If someone strikes me on one cheek, I should turn the other cheek to him?

Father: I'm supposed to let someone take both my cloak and my tunic?

Narrator: People would listen for hours until Jesus would go off to pray or rest or move on to the next town.

Daughter: That sure was an earful, wasn't it?

Son: Yeah, remember that Jesus said we are to let our light shine before men, that they may see our good deeds and praise God!

Daughter: And then, our reward will be great.

Mother: It sounds like Jesus is talking about not only a great kingdom, but a home for everybody.

Challenges

The Beatitudes

Though the family in today's drama is fictional, the teachings are real, as is the dilemma of trying to remember all that Jesus taught. Having a constant reminder is a good start toward creating the familiarity that will help the children teach others.

Have children copy the Beatitudes from a larger copy you have displayed. Allow them to decorate the verses as they wish. Encourage them to take home and display the verses in a place where they can be reminded of what Jesus said in the Beatitudes.

Matthew 5:3–11

Blessed are the poor in spirit, for theirs is the kingdom of heaven.

Blessed are those who mourn, for they will be comforted.

Blessed are the meek, for they will inherit the earth.

Blessed are those who hunger and thirst for righteousness, for they will be filled.

Blessed are the merciful, for they will be shown mercy.

Blessed are the pure in heart, for they will see God.

Blessed are the peacemakers, for they will be called sons of God.

Blessed are those who are persecuted because of righteousness, for theirs is the kingdom of heaven.

Blessed are you when people insult you, persecute you and falsely say all kinds of evil against you because of me.

The "Do to Others" Challenge!

Help children explore the applications of "do to others as you would have them do to you" (Matthew 7:12) by filling in the blanks of the following sentence:

I will treat ________________ like I wish to be
(person)

treated by ______________________________.
(thoughtful action)

(For example: I will treat my brother Max like I wish to be treated by inviting him to play soccer.)

Write the sentence where everyone can see it. Form a circle and give each child a chance to complete the sentence by naming a person in the first blank and a thoughtful action in the second.

To make the exercise both challenging and fun, have children see how many times they can go around the circle without anyone repeating an action. Alternatively, see how quickly they can complete one time around.

Be sure to allow time for discussion on how these actions will make them teachers of the message that Jesus shared.

A Healer

Jesus healed the sick and brought the dead back to life. In addition to the words He spoke, Jesus's very presence gave people hope and healing. Most importantly, Jesus's death and resurrection revealed the larger message that He had won, for all of us, victory over death itself.

Through prayer and confidence in God's Word, we, too, are healers. *Ask and you shall receive, and your joy will be complete.* (John 16:24) But, how can we explain to children when healing doesn't come as we would like or when someone they have lost does not come back to life? We can encourage children to continue to base their beliefs on God's Word rather than their own or anyone else's experiences.

Children can also be healers through kindness, thoughtfulness, and by being good listeners. Some people do see and feel healing in the smallest gestures, words, or hope brought to them in a time of sorrow or illness.

We should act boldly as healers, believing that God will hear our prayers and answer them. It is what Jesus demonstrated with His life. It's how we can participate like Jesus, as a healer, in God's world.

Jesus Brings Lazarus Back to Life

Learn more in John 11:1–44

Assign readers for the characters listed below.

Narrator

Man

Woman

Martha

Jesus

Mary

Narrator: Martha and her sister Mary sent a message to Jesus asking Him to come quickly, for their brother Lazarus was sick and needed healing. However, it was several days before Jesus arrived in Bethany where they lived. Many people were now visiting the house to comfort Mary and Martha because Lazarus was dead. Martha went out to greet Jesus as he entered the town.

Man: I'm sorry about your brother, Martha.

Woman: You cared for him as best you could.

Martha: Thank you. Oh, Jesus, you're finally here!

Jesus: Greetings, Martha.

Martha: My brother has died. I know that, had You been here sooner, he would not have died. But, I know God will give You whatever you ask.

Jesus: Martha, your brother will rise from the dead.

Martha: Yes, I know the Scriptures tell us we will all rise at the resurrection.

Jesus: But, you see, I am the resurrection and the life. He who believes in Me will live. Whoever lives and believes in Me will never die. Do you believe this is true?

Martha: Jesus, I believe You are the Christ, the Son of God! I believe that You are the One the world has been waiting for.

Narrator: Martha returned home and told Mary that Jesus had arrived. Mary seemed disappointed with Jesus.

Mary: Oh, Jesus, if you had only been here sooner, our brother would still be alive.

Jesus: Take me to where he is.

Narrator: The sisters took Jesus to Lazarus's tomb. When he got there, Jesus wept because He truly loved Lazarus. He approached the tomb, which had a large stone in front of it.

Jesus: Take away the stone!

Martha: No, Jesus, he has been in there too long.

Jesus: Didn't I tell you that if you only had faith, you would see the glory of the Lord?

Narrator: The stone was rolled away. Then, Jesus prayed. He knew God heard all of His prayers, but He prayed again so that people would see that what was about to happen was a sign that Jesus was indeed sent by God.

Jesus: Thank You, Father, for hearing my prayers.

Narrator: And then, in a loud voice, Jesus called—

Jesus: Lazarus, come out!

Narrator: From the opening in the tomb, Lazarus appeared! He was alive!

Jesus: Take those grave clothes off him. Let him go.

Narrator: Lazarus's resurrection brought joy to his family and caused many to believe that Jesus was the Son of God.

Challenges

Share: A Miracle in My Life

Ask children about a time in their lives when they believe a miracle occurred. Do not limit them to healing stories for the purpose of this exercise—any miracle will do. Ask them to explain why they believe the event was a miracle. Sometimes, we do not see the miraculous until it is recognized and named as such.

If the group is slow to think of examples, recount a miracle in your life, one that has happened in the church community, or a miracle you heard about on the news.

Prayer List

Teach children the importance of praying for others. Encourage them to pray for each other in class, anointing each other's heads with olive oil. Another good practice to adopt is keeping a prayer list of people who are sick, in the hospital, or just going through a rough time. When children are praying with others, instruct them to anoint the head of the other person(s) with olive oil.

Jesus instructed the 12 disciples to preach to others and to heal them. The disciples "anointed many sick people with oil and healed them" (Mark 6:13). Remember, Jesus *instructed* His disciples to pray for others. He has instructed us to do the same because we are His disciples as well.

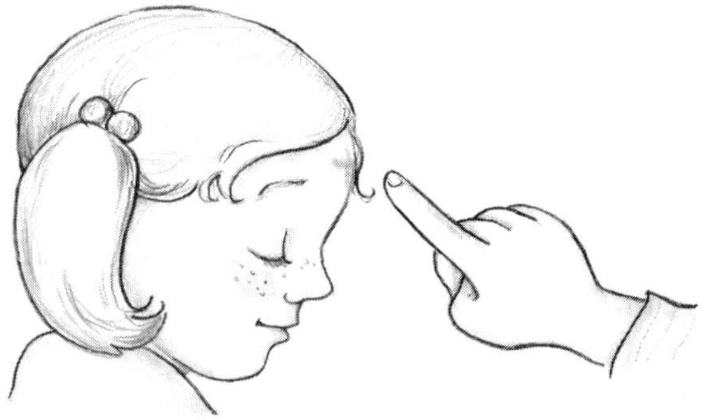

Prayer Cards

Being a healer doesn't mean we have to be the ones who provide the ultimate act of healing. That is God's role in the process. We can pray and do other things to help heal others.

After you've taught children to keep prayer lists, as a class, create a prayer card for each person on the lists. Each card's prayer doesn't need to be long, involved, or even particularly perfect language. What matters is that it is the prayer the children are praying. The people receiving the cards will not only have the reassurance that others are remembering them, they will see what happens when people are praying for them.

The prayer could be as simple as this:

Father, we are glad that You hear us when we pray. Please bless Mr. Anderson with your presence. He is sick with pneumonia and needs our prayers and Your healing touch. Amen.

Sending these prayer cards signed by the children will bring a moment of grace in lives in need of healing.

A Servant

Jesus was what? A servant? But, He was the Son of God; He should have been served. However, being served wasn't the point of Jesus's ministry or of His life. He explained this to the disciples when some began asking for special treatment. . . .*and whoever wants to be first must be your slave—just as the Son of Man did not come to be served, but to serve, and to give his life as a ransom for many.* Matthew 20:27–28

Indeed, Jesus's teaching was service, His miracles were service, and even His death and resurrection were acts of service. But, to people who were waiting for the Messiah, this image did not match that of the mighty conqueror they assumed was coming. Jesus *was* the Messiah. But, He didn't hold onto His status. Instead, He humbled Himself and became a servant to many (Philippians 2:6–7).

Jesus even performed what seemed to be a lowly act of service. During the time Jesus lived on Earth, people wore sandals or walked barefoot everywhere they went. People would call on their lowliest servants to wash the dirt from their feet at the end of the day. However, Jesus wrapped a towel around His waist and washed His disciples' feet (John 13:1–17). What a lowly task for the Messiah!

Jesus humbled Himself to serve others even though He was God's Son. What is important to remember is that we should never think of ourselves as better than someone else. Instead, we should be like Jesus— always ready and willing to serve. *Each of you should look not only to your own interests, but also to the interests of others.* Philippians 2:4

Jesus Washes the Disciples' Feet

Learn more in John 13:1–17.

Assign readers for the characters listed below.

Narrator

Peter

Jesus

Narrator: Jesus and His disciples gathered to share the Passover meal. When the meal was being served, Jesus got up from where He was seated, put a towel around His waist, and filled a basin with water.

Peter: Lord, what are you doing?

Narrator: Jesus had surprised His disciples many times with the things He had said and done. But this one act on the night before He was crucified, would show the disciples what it was that Jesus had been trying to teach them.

Jesus: Peter, I am going to wash your feet. In fact, I am going to wash the feet of everyone here so that you may be clean.

Peter: No, you are not!

Jesus: You don't realize what I am doing now, but later, you will.

Peter: No, Lord, I cannot have You washing my feet! It's not right; you are my Lord, my Teacher, my Master.

Jesus: But, Peter, unless you let me wash your feet, you can't really be a part of what I have been teaching you, about what God wants for this world.

Peter: All I have to do is get my feet washed?

Jesus: Yes.

Peter: Well, then, wash my feet, Lord and don't stop there; wash my hands and my head as well. I want to be clean all over.

Jesus: Peter, people who have taken a bath are clean. Only their feet need to be washed. You are clean now that yours have been washed.

Narrator: Jesus continued around the table washing the disciples' feet. When He was done, He returned to His place among them.

Jesus: Do you understand what I have just done? You are right to call me Lord and to call me Teacher. But, now your Lord and your Teacher has washed your feet. Do as I have done.

Narrator: Jesus knew the time had come for Him to return to His Father who had sent Him and had given Him the power to do all that He had done.

Jesus: Listen, the messenger is never greater than the one who sends the message. No servant is greater than his master. Go and do the things I have shown you and you will be blessed!

Challenges

Service Circle
Help children relate to the story of Jesus washing the disciples' feet through this exercise. Have children form a circle. Tell them to take their shoes off and place them behind where they are sitting.

Now, give each child a few baby wipes. Have each child take a turn washing the feet of the person to her right. Go all around the circle, encouraging each child to pay attention to the act being performed.

By the time the circle is completed, each child will have had a turn to serve and to be served. Discuss the exercise: How did it feel to be served like this? How did you feel as you served your neighbor?

Class Service Project
Is your class involved in a group service project? If not, choose a long-term, recurring project, like helping at a homeless shelter or working at a food bank. Perhaps you can pick up trash in the parking lot or help out with coffee hour or in the nursery on Sundays. Do something that will give a sense of completion. Then, talk about what was learned from even a small act of service. Helping in the nursery one Sunday may not help the world, but that wasn't what Jesus was teaching when He washed the feet of His disciples. Instead, talk about how offering to serve, helps us become more like Jesus. He chose to serve God by serving God's people with His life.

Service List
Help children take this lesson out of the classroom and into their homes. Have children list the chores they are responsible for at home. They should make their lists exhaustive, even down to making their beds.

Then, have children list the chores their siblings and parents do. These do not need to be categorized by person, but simply chores that other people do to make the home a better place. Again, the lists should be as exhaustive as possible, including the biggest thing to the smallest.

Finally, have children pick a few activities from the lists of chores their siblings and parents do. Tell them to volunteer to do these chores—if only just once. Help them choose things they are likely to follow up on—no volunteering to pay the mortgage!

Explain that serving is not just doing what is expected of us, but going beyond to where we are actually helping others directly with their needs. Also, explain that as we serve, we should focus on others and not ourselves. The attitude of service is just as important as the act itself. Challenge children to follow through on their service activities.

Obedient to God's Will

On the night of the Passover meal, Jesus knew His "appointed time was near" (Matthew 26:18). During the meal, Jesus broke bread and told the disciples to take and eat it, for it was His body (Matthew 26:26). *Then he took the cup, gave thanks and offered it to them, saying, "Drink from it, all of you. This is my blood of the covenant, which is poured out for many for the forgiveness of sins."* Matthew 26:27–28 Jesus knew that He was getting ready to pay the price for all sin. He was about to give up His own life so that through Him, we could have eternal life. However, Jesus had to pray that God's will would be done and not His own (Mark 14:36).

After Judas left the group to complete his act of betrayal, the other disciples accompanied Jesus to the Garden of Gethsemane. They fell asleep shortly after their arrival. Jesus knew that the next day held terrible things in store for Him: persecution, torture, and finally death. We can't help but be amazed by Jesus's willingness to follow through with God's will.

Jesus showed obedience every day of His life. In the hours of prayer in the Garden of Gethsemane, we see that this is indeed a difficult period for Him, He asks three times for God to "take this cup" from Him (Mark 14:36). Even though He was the Son of God, Jesus wasn't immune to the physical and emotional pain of facing death. *Yet not what I will, but what you will.* (Mark 14:36) This is Jesus's powerful prayer of obedience. We should also be obedient and surrender our will in favor of God's.

Jesus told the disciples to eat the bread and drink from the cup in remembrance of Him. (Luke 22:19 KJV) We, too, are to remember how He was obedient by surrendering to God's will and not to His own. Two thousand years later, we still benefit from that action and will continue to do so into eternity. We should also be obedient to God's perfect will. What better way to be like Jesus than to be obedient to God?

Jesus in the Garden

Learn more in Matthew 26:36–42, Mark 14:32-36, Luke 22:39–44

Assign readers for the characters listed below.

Narrator

Jesus

Peter

Narrator: On the night of his arrest, Jesus and several of His disciples traveled to the Garden of Gethsemane. Judas was also on his way to this place, but he was guiding the authorities who would ultimately arrest Jesus.

Jesus: Men, sit here while I go and pray. Peter, James, John, would you come with Me?

Narrator: As the three men followed Him, Jesus began to feel troubled.

Jesus: Peter, James, and John, My soul is filled with a great sorrow. Please, stay here with Me and keep watch as I pray.

Narrator: Then, as He had so many times in His life, Jesus went off by Himself to pray to God.

Jesus: Father, all things are possible for You. If there is a way, take this cup from Me. But Father, I must do what You want, not what I want.

Narrator: Then, Jesus found Peter sleeping.

Jesus: Peter, are all of you sleeping? Couldn't you stay awake and keep watch for Me for even one hour?

Peter: We wanted to, but we were so tired, Lord.

Jesus: Yes, our spirits want one thing, but our bodies want another. Our bodies are weak that way. Please, keep watch as I pray.

Peter: Yes, Jesus.

Jesus: Father, I am so troubled. I ask that You spare Me from this sacrifice, yet I know that what You have planned is best.

Narrator: Once again, Jesus checked on the disciples, but they were asleep. Once again, He returned to prayer.

Jesus: Father, even with the trouble I feel in my soul, even though I ask to be spared this cup, I say not what I will, but what You will!

Narrator: A crowd was approaching Gethsemane as Jesus woke the sleeping disciples.

Jesus: Asleep again? Listen, the time has come for Me to be betrayed by a friend and given over to the hands of sinners. Here they are. Come, let us go!

Narrator: With that, Jesus showed His obedience to God's will and walked into the arms of those who wanted to kill Him.

Challenges

I Will What God Wills

Jesus demonstrated a great prayer when He prayed in the Garden of Gethsemane. *Yet not what I will, but what you will.* (Mark 14:36) This prayer hands everything over to God.

Most pictures of Jesus praying in the garden show Him kneeling with His folded hands on a rock. If you can find such a picture, show it to children before doing this project. You can also display the picture on page 40.

Have children create rocks from bakeable or self-hardening clay. They should make a flat surface on the top of each rock. Then, with an etching tool, have them carve the following verse.

Yet not what I will, but what you will.
Mark 14:36

When the rocks have been baked or have hardened, have children take the rocks home to remind them to pray just as Jesus did.

Share: Tell a Time It Was Hard to Obey

Sometimes, it is hard to be obedient to an authority figure. Have children talk about a time they found it hard to obey a rule, either at home or at school. What lesson did they learn? Did they obey or disobey? What trouble did they avoid by obeying or experience by disobeying?

The Greatest Commandment

Knowing God's will for every circumstance can be difficult, but certainly, God's Word holds the key. Jesus said that the first and greatest commandment is to "love your God with all your heart, soul, and mind." He continued with the second greatest commandment: to "love your neighbor as yourself" (Matthew 22:37–39).

Obeying God, then, starts with loving God with all of your heart, soul, and mind. What does it mean to love with heart, soul, and mind? Well, the phrase "heart, soul, and mind" is another way of saying "with everything you've got!" Have children come up with ways they can enthusiastically show their love for God.

Loving God with our hearts means that God should be the center of our love and joy. We should love Him with our whole hearts so that we can express the love God has for us by showing others the same love. Loving God with our souls means that we should express this love in spirit and in truth. In other words, we are to worship God honestly. And, finally, loving God with our minds means that we should show our love for Him through what we say and by reading and learning His Word. Have children write down the many ways they can love God with their hearts, souls, and minds.

A Living Sacrifice

For God so loved the world that
He gave His one and only Son. John 3:16

The story of Jesus's crucifixion is the story we most readily associate with this verse. Jesus sacrificed His life so that we could live forever with God. To sacrifice means to take something highly valued and to put it to the side for the sake of something else that has a greater value. Take some time to reflect on that definition of the word "sacrifice" and on John 3:16. Just think, God loved us so much, that He gave us His highly valued Son so that we could have something of great value—eternal life. Jesus certainly sacrificed His life on the cross. However, the sacrifice actually began much earlier, approximately 33 years earlier.

From the moment He was recognized as the Messiah by Simeon in the Temple (Luke 2:21–40), Jesus's whole life was given over to preparing for and carrying out His life of ministry. We don't know much about His childhood, but we do know from the Gospels that Jesus didn't spend time thinking about Himself. Jesus spent His life being a living sacrifice by teaching, praying for, healing, and giving to others.

The apostle Paul provides much of the biblical text in the New Testament. Paul seems to really understand what Jesus was teaching, and he urges his audience in Romans 12:1 to offer themselves as "living sacrifices, holy and pleasing to God." Paul preached the same selflessness that Jesus modeled. It is a selflessness that we, too, can adopt and teach children to adopt in order to become more like Jesus.

We can also offer ourselves as living sacrifices by setting aside our own needs for the sake of others. Giving to someone doesn't just mean giving a tangible gift. We can give by offering ears to listen, arms to embrace, and a voice to speak words of encouragement. We can act as living sacrifices by spending time with those who may be in need of a friend. We should willingly visit those who are in the hospital or a nursing home. Spending time with those whose families can't be present shows that someone else is thinking of them.

Jesus was a living sacrifice for us as He lived His life serving others and fulfilling God's plan. Instead of worrying about our own needs and what we have to accomplish on our "To Do" lists, we should live like Jesus—sacrificing ourselves to pray for, serve, encourage, and care for others.

Jesus on the Cross

Learn more in Luke 23:26–53.

Assign readers for the characters listed below.

Narrator

The Crowd (the entire class)

Jesus

Ruler

Criminal 1

Criminal 2

Centurion

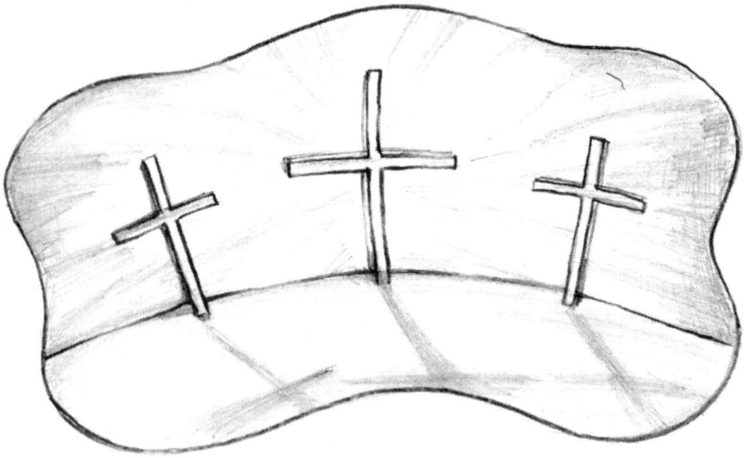

Narrator: Pilate wanted to release Jesus from custody. However, the people turned against Him and requested the release of Barabbas, a murderer, instead of Jesus. In one voice, the crowd shouted—

The Crowd: Crucify Him! Crucify Him!

Narrator: And, with that, Jesus was taken away to be crucified. Jesus was nailed to a cross and placed beside two criminals. Even there the people continued to mock Him.

Jesus: Father, forgive them for they do not know what they are doing.

Ruler: He saved others; let Him save Himself if He is the Christ, the Chosen One!

Narrator: Even one of the criminals beside Jesus mocked Him.

Criminal 1: Aren't You the Christ? Save Yourself and us!

Criminal 2: Don't you fear God? We are getting what we deserve. This man did nothing wrong. Jesus, please remember me when you enter into Your Kingdom.

Jesus: Today, you will be with Me in Paradise.

Narrator: Darkness then fell on the land, and the curtain on the Temple was torn in two.

Jesus: Father, I commit My Spirit into Your hands.

Narrator: Jesus breathed His last breath. One man, standing by the cross, realized who Jesus truly was.

Centurion: Surely, this was a righteous man.

Narrator: A man named Joseph went to Pilate and asked for the body of Jesus. Joseph wrapped Jesus's body in a linen cloth and placed Him in a tomb cut in rock. But, just as Jesus foretold, He rose from the dead, and His body would not be found where Joseph placed it.

Challenges

Prayer of Thanksgiving

There is a great moment in Jesus's life when He has just healed ten men of leprosy, and they all head off to new lives, most likely caught up in the excitement of being free from such an awful disease. One of the men suddenly remembers something; he runs back and thanks Jesus. "Thank you, Jesus" he says, "for new life."

Read this story to children, from Luke 17:11–19. It is a great reminder of all of the things Jesus did for us throughout His lifetime and through His death. Then lead children in a prayer giving thanks to Jesus for being a healer, a teacher, a friend, a servant, and a living sacrifice.

Time Share

Children can be living sacrifices just as Jesus was. Remember, Jesus spent His entire life serving others. Teach children the importance of putting others before themselves. Through giving their time and sharing their gifts with others, they are acting as living sacrifices.

Invite children to brainstorm ways they can be living sacrifices for their family, friends, and communities. Some ways can be: cooking food with an adult to take to a shelter, baking cookies to give to those who are working long hours at a hospital, collecting clothes and toys to give to needy children, visiting and praying for the sick, and spending time reading and playing board games with the elderly in nursing homes.

Have children select ways they can be living sacrifices. Then, have them pair up with an adult who will help them with whatever they need, whether it's driving them to where they need to go, helping them cook, or gathering items to give away. Adults will be their accountability partners. Whichever way they decide to give their time, share with children that they are living like Jesus by offering themselves as living sacrifices, just as Jesus did for all of us.

Walking in His Light

But if we walk in the light, as he is in the light, we have fellowship with one another, and the blood of Jesus, his Son, purifies us from all sin. (1 John 1:7)

Just as the Scriptures predicted, the Messiah came (Isaiah 9:1–7). He taught, He healed, and He died in order to defeat death for us. He then rose from the dead.

As we see by the reaction of many of the disciples after Jesus's death, they had trouble accepting the news that Jesus had risen. Two of the disciples were walking to a village called Emmaus. They were grieving because they thought the Messiah was dead. They didn't understand that Jesus had to die so that he could rise again to fulfill the Scriptures.

While they walked, Jesus appeared to the mourning disciples on the road to Emmaus. He took the time to put His life and death into the context of Scripture, teaching them and walking with them.

That evening, Jesus ate with the two men. When Jesus broke the bread, the men's eyes were opened! They recognized the man that walked with them as Jesus, and their mourning was turned to joy! The two men went back to Jerusalem, excited about the news that Jesus had risen. They couldn't wait to spread the news to the other disciples so that they, too, could be filled with joy and hope.

To be like Jesus, then, is to be committed to walking alongside others, even in tough times. We must let them know that there is a bigger story that we are a part of, one that is characterized by the good news that Jesus Christ rose again. We are to walk in Jesus's light just as the disciples did when they found out He had risen from the dead. We are to renew the joy of others by spreading the good news of salvation.

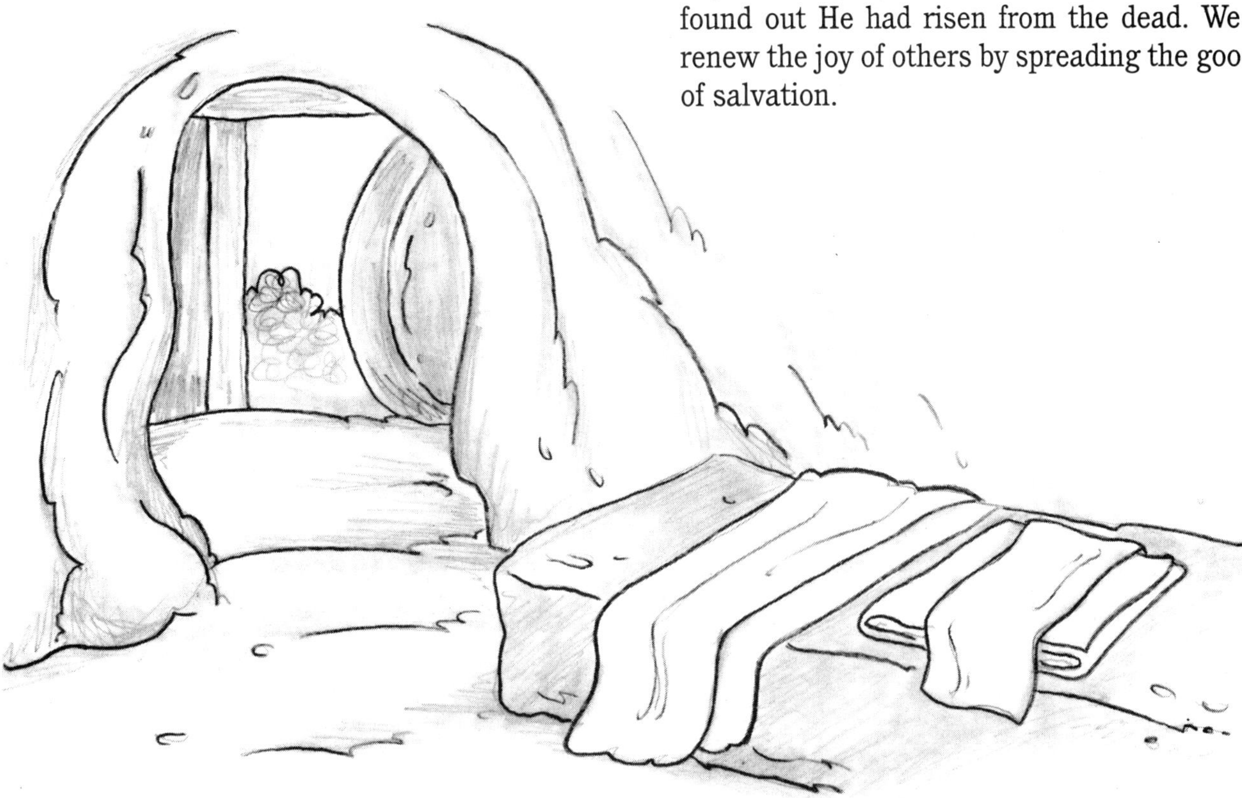

On the Road to Emmaus

Learn more in the Luke 24:13–53.

Assign readers for the characters listed below.

Narrator

Man 1

Man 2

Jesus/Man on the Road

Narrator: Three days after the death of Jesus, two of the disciples were walking from Jerusalem to the town of Emmaus. Their hearts were filled with sadness.

Man 1: It seems this road is harder to travel when we are carrying the weight of such bad news.

Man 2: That is so true. Still, night is approaching, and we must continue.

Man 1: And I'm so hungry.

Man 2: Who would ever have thought that things would go so badly for us.

Man 1: For us and all of Israel!

Man 2: It's just that He really seemed to be the Messiah. The miracles He performed, the things He said . . .

Man 1: . . . and even the way He said them. It was as if Jesus of Nazareth was speaking the words of God Himself!

Man 2: Now, we find ourselves once again hoping for the future, even while feeling so hopeless.

Jesus/Man on the Road: Excuse me, gentlemen, I did not mean to be listening to your conversation, but you sound so sad. Tell me, what is the trouble?

Man 2: Have you not heard?

Jesus/Man on the Road: Heard what?

Man 1: The events of the past few days.

Man 2: Everyone is talking about it!

Man 1: Well, walk with us and we'll tell you everything.

Man 2: Jesus of Nazareth, the One we had hoped was the Messiah, was crucified.

Man 1: We must have been wrong about Him.

Jesus/Man on the Road: I know that the Jews have been waiting for someone to come and save them for many, many years. You see, I am a Jew, and I know what the Scriptures predicted.

Man 2: Perhaps, you know something we do not?

Jesus/Man on the Road: I know that if you go back as far as the writings of Moses, a Savior is promised to come. I know that this Jesus you are speaking of fulfilled the many prophecies that foretold the coming of the Messiah.

Man 1: Such as?

Jesus/Man on the Road: Such as the fact that He was born of a virgin in Bethlehem and that He would go into hiding in Egypt but return to preach, to teach, and to heal.

Man 1: Yes, yes, but He was arrested and crucified.

Man 2: Then buried. Some of our women claim that when they went to His tomb, it was empty. Angels told them that Jesus was alive.

Man 1: But, some of our men went looking for Jesus and did not find Him anywhere.

Jesus/Man on the Road: Don't you see? That, too, was just as the prophets said it would be.

Man 1: Well, we've arrived. Listen, it's getting dark. You can't continue on the road alone. Join us for some supper.

Man 2: Yes, please join us.

Narrator: The man joined them. He took bread, blessed and broke it. That's when the men realized that it was Jesus who was with them. Immediately, Jesus disappeared from their sight.

Man 1: The man on the road, He . . .

Man 2: . . . He was Jesus, He *is* Jesus. He's alive!

Man 1: Our journey began with what we thought was bad news, but Jesus came and showed us that it was, in fact, the good news!

Narrator: The two men went on to find the rest of the disciples and told them that the Lord had risen. Just then, someone said . . .

Jesus/Man on the Road: . . . Peace be with you. Remember, the Scriptures had to be fulfilled. They said the Christ would suffer much but will rise from the dead on the third day. Forgiveness of sins will be preached everywhere in His name.

Narrator: Jesus then blessed the eleven disciples, and He was taken up into heaven. The disciples returned to the Temple in Jerusalem where they praised God for the Messiah.

Challenges

The Reason for the Hope

The Apostle Peter wrote, *always be prepared to give an answer to everyone who asks you to give a reason for the hope that you have.* 1 Peter 3:15 Peter's words encourage us to be like Jesus on the road to Emmaus and to be able to articulate the story that is central to our faith.

Have children role-play with you so that they can practice sharing the good news. Pretend that you have never heard of Jesus. What kinds of things would children want you to know? Encourage them to offer everything they know and be ready to fill in any gaps.

As Christians, we need to let our lights shine by teaching and encouraging others to believe that Jesus has risen. We should live like we believe that Jesus is alive and our hope is in Him.

Brainstorm: What Does It Mean in Your Life?

What better way to win someone over to Christ than by showing them how He has changed your life? When people look at you, they should see the Lord's light shining all over you. This means, that when someone is around you, there shouldn't be any doubt that you are indeed a follower of Christ.

For some, it isn't easy to believe that Christ rose from the dead. For some, it's even harder to follow the teachings of Jesus Christ. Just think of how easy life would be if everyone in the world was a Christian. Unfortunately, this isn't the case. It is up to us, as Christians, to lead by example.

Take just one line from the Sermon on the Mount Matthew 5:14 *You are the light of the world.* This gives us the responsibility and privilege of showing people to God by the way we live. Brainstorm with children ways they can let their lights shine.